THE RUN-AWAY DRINK BOTTLES

ISBN:9781916554153

By sylvia Baker

In a school classroom, sat many colorful and shiny drink bottles neatly lined up on a table. They were filled with water, juice, and other refreshing drinks for the children to enjoy during lunchtime.

The drink bottles were not happy.

Every time the children took a sip from them, they would bite the bottles with their sharp teeth. It was painful and uncomfortable for the bottles, and they had had enough.

One day, while the children were chattering and playing the drink bottles saw an opportunity to escape.

They wobbled and rolled off the shelf and onto the classroom floor, quickly scurrying towards the door.

The children didn't notice the drink bottles running away at first, but soon they realized that their drinks were missing.

They looked around the classroom and saw the empty table and the open door.

The children Looked for their drink bottles everywhere but could not find them.

The children were so thirsty that they felt like they were going to faint.

They couldn't think of a reason why their drink bottles would do such a thing.

So they decided to see if they could find a trail. .
Soon they had turned into detectives.

Where could the drink bottles be?

Think of places they could have gone.

After a long long time of searching and feeling thirsty.

The children found their bottles in the playground.

"Why did you all run away, the children asked?"

The drink bottles spoke up, "We are tired of being bitten every time you drink from us. It hurts, and we don't like it. We just want to be used and enjoyed without any pain."

"We are so Sorry."

The children felt ashamed 🪣 and guilty for their actions. They realized that they had been mistreating the drink bottles. And they promised to be more careful in the future.

From that day on, the children treated the drink bottles with care and respect, and the bottles were happy to provide them with refreshing drinks without any pain.

The drink bottles had finally found peace.

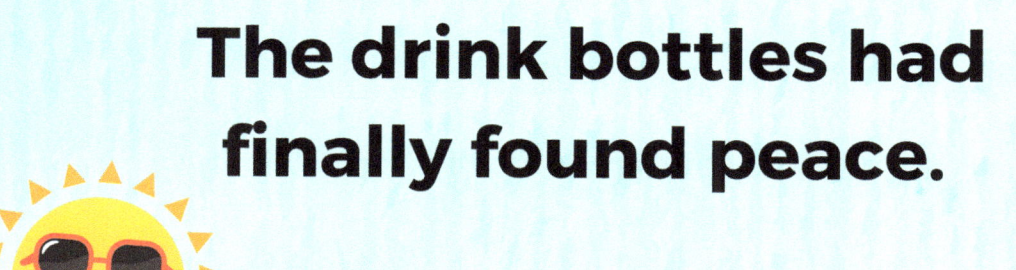

The story teaches.

An adult could help with the rest of these passages.

The story of the drink bottles that ran away from a school classroom before lunchtime is a lesson in empathy and respect. It encourages us to treat the objects in our lives with the care that they deserve, recognizing that they deserve to be treated with kindness. This simple story teaches us a valuable lesson that we can all carry with us throughout our lives.

How could the children convince the bottles to come back to them?

If the children wanted to convince the drink bottles to come back, they would need to show the bottles that they were truly sorry for mistreating them and that they were committed to treating them with care.

The children could start by apologizing to the drink bottles and acknowledging the pain and discomfort they had caused them. They could then explain how they would change their behavior, such as being more gentle when drinking from the bottles and ensuring that they were not biting.

To show their commitment to treating the drink bottles with care, the children could offer to decorate them with stickers or markers to make them feel special and valued.

They could also offer to clean the bottles regularly, ensuring that they were always hygienic and free from any bacteria or germs which keeps bugging the drink bottles at night.

They could also acknowledge how the drink bottles are an important part of their daily routine and how much they valued having them in their classroom.

By taking these steps, the children would demonstrate to the drink bottles that they were sincere in their apology and committed to treating them with the care they deserved. With time and patience, the drink bottles would provide the children with refreshing drinks once again.

what is the best way to say sorry or apologize if you have wronged someone?

When you have wronged someone, it is important to apologize sincerely and take responsibility for your actions. Here are some steps to help you apologize:

Acknowledge your mistake:
Start by acknowledging what you did wrong and take responsibility for your actions. Be specific about what you did and how it impacted the other person.

Express remorse: Show that you are genuinely sorry and empathize with how your actions have affected the other person. Use words like "I'm sorry," "I regret what I did," or "I feel terrible about what happened."

Change your behavior: Explain how you plan to change your behavior in the future to ensure that the same mistake won't happen again.

Make a plan to avoid repeating the same mistake.

Give the other person time and space:

Understand that the person may need some time and space to process what happened and come to terms with your apology.

Respect their wishes and give them the time they need.

Remember that a sincere apology requires more than just saying "I'm sorry." It requires humility, empathy, and a willingness to make things right.

By taking responsibility for your actions, expressing genuine remorse, and making amends, you can show the other person that you are truly sorry for what happened and are committed to making things right

Dedication

To my daughter RACHEL
I love you so much.

www.ingramcontent.com/pod-product-compliance
Lightning Source LLC
Chambersburg PA
CBHW051321110526
44590CB00031B/4431